D0612692

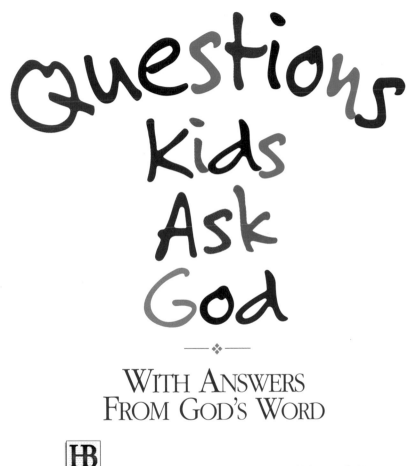

Questions Kids Ask God

WITH ANSWERS
FROM GOD'S WORD

HB HONOR BOOKS · Honor Books • P.O. Box 55388 • Tulsa, Oklahoma 74155

4TH Printing

Scripture quotations marked ICB are taken from the *International Children's Bible,* New Century Version, copyright © 1986, 1988 by Word Publishing, Dallas, Texas 75039. Used by permission.

Verses marked TLB are taken from *The Living Bible,* copyright © 1971. Used by permission of Tyndale House Publishers, Inc., Wheaton, Illinois 60198.

Scripture quotations marked NAS are taken from *The New American Standard Bible,* copyright © 1977 by The Lockman Foundation 1960, 1962, 1963, 1968, 1971, 1972, 1973, 1975, 1977. Used by permission.

Scripture quotations marked NKJV are taken from *The New King James Version* of the Bible, copyright © 1979, 1980, 1982, 1983, 1984 by Thomas Nelson, Inc. Publishers. Used by permission.

Questions Kids Ask God With Answers From God's Word
ISBN 1-56292-069-3
Copyright © 1995 by Honor Books
P.O. Box 55388
Tulsa, Oklahoma 74155

Published by Honor Books
P.O. Box 55388
Tulsa, Oklahoma, 74155

Manuscript compiled by
W. B. Freeman Concepts, Inc.
Tulsa, Oklahoma

Questions from a Pure Heart

W e've all heard the phrase "out of the mouths of babes" to refer to the uncontrived, spontaneous ability of children to express truth when adults don't dare to do so! This book may very well have been titled "Questions about Life, God, and Heaven — Out of the Mouths of Babes!"

Questions Kids Ask God is a refreshingly candid collection of real questions asked by real children about real life. It presents some ponderings that adults may not always speak as candidly or openly about, but no doubt mull over secretly in the childlike nooks of their own hearts.

A pure heart knows no fear. And an innocent heart is capable of asking the unanswerable. Indeed, many of the questions asked here are questions that virtually everybody has asked at some time in their own way. They are a reflection of pure, innocent hearts — unembarrassed by their own naivete, and equally unaware of the profound nature of their queries.

Children's questions touch upon the mystery of God. They address the Lord who has not revealed Himself fully to man, for man's sake . . . the Almighty King of the Universe whose splendor and infinite power are beyond mankind's ability to grasp. They bring a pure innocence to our thinking about the Omniscient and Holy One who alone sees the beginning from the ending and yet knows every detail of His creation at each moment in eternity.

A young child, of course, doesn't want to hear about the *mystery* of God. Children are "concrete thinkers" — they deal in the here and now and with what can be experienced by the senses. They want answers that are plain, simple, direct, and immediate, even though they ask questions that are often anything but simple and concrete!

At the same time, virtually every child understands what it means to "have a secret." The best answer to many of the questions in this book is this: "I don't know. God hasn't told us that secret yet."

In other cases, God's Word provides clear answers to the questions we ask. When a verse or two of Scripture seems appropriate as an answer to a child's question, we have provided it. Certainly when taken as a whole, God's Word provides answers to the deepest desires and most important questions we can ask. To discover those answers, however, requires consistent reading and contemplation of the Scriptures *in their entirety.* We encourage you to spend time each day reading God's Word *with* your child. You'll discover answers to questions your child has asked, is asking, and has yet to ask!

By all means, we encourage you to be honest with your child and to *not* attempt to answer the questions for which you have no answer. If you don't know, or don't know how to express an answer at a level your child can understand, admit that to your child. Your child will respect you more, not less, and actually take comfort in the fact that nobody has all the answers all the time. You should feel free to say to your child, "I've wondered that myself," or "That's a great question. I trust the Lord will give both of us the answer to that question some day."

Let these questions speak to *your* heart. The search for truth very often begins with childlike questions. Jesus said it best:

> "Ask, and it will be given to you; seek, and
> you will find; knock, and it will be opened to you.
> For everyone who asks receives, and he who seeks finds,
> and to him who knocks it will be opened."
>
> MATTHEW 7:7-8 (NKJV)

Dear God,
How did you make our
hair?

Andrew
(age 6)

I praise you because you
made me in an amazing and wonderful way.

PSALM 139:14 (ICB)

Dear God,

Will there be baseball in heaven? Because if there isn't I don't know if I want to go. I really love baseball!

Andy (age 9)

Lord our God . . . your plans for us are many.
If I tried to tell them all, there would be too many to count.

PSALM 40:5 (ICB)

Dear God,

Is there going to be my grandpa Dick in heaven? Because I have never seen him in my life.

Paige (age 9)

Dear God,
What is heaven REALLY like? I've heard different theories.

Marus (age 10)

"The Paradise of God"

REVELATION 2:7 (TLB)

Dear God,
Will there be petstores
in heaven? If there are
I want to get a golden
retrevir puppy.

Abigail (age 8)

Day by day the Lord observes the good deeds
done by godly men, and gives them eternal rewards.

PSALM 37:18 (TLB)

Dear God,
   Is there hockey in heaven? I hope so, because the angels would be good goalies. I hope I can beat them.

JOSEPH
(age 5)

Dear God,

My parents are divorced. Which family will I live with in heaven.

Love,
Jonathan (age 8)

For in the resurrection
they neither marry, nor are given in marriage,
but are like angels in heaven.

MATTHEW 22: 30 (NAS)

Dear God,
How did you get to be so big? How can you hold the earth in your hands? I can't even hold a globe in my hands.

Chris (Age 9)

The Lord is great.
He is worthy of our praise.
No one can understand how great he is.

PSALM 145:3 (ICB)

Dear God,
How do you listen to all those churches praying at one time?

Margaret (age 8)

The Lord sees the good people.
He listens to their prayers.

PSALM 34:15 (ICB)

Dear God,

Will there ever be peace again? I would really like to know.

Jessi (age 10)

And they will hammer their swords into plowshares,
and their spears into pruning hooks.
Nation will not lift up sword against nation,
and never again will they learn war.

ISAIAH 2:4 (NAS)

Dear God,

Why did you write such a big book of long verses? You know--the Bible, We have to learn very long verses,

Jeff (age 10)

The whole Bible was given to us by inspiration from God and is useful to teach us what is true and to make us realize what is wrong in our lives; it straightens us out and helps us do what is right.

2 TIMOTHY 3:16 (TLB)

DEAR GOD,
IF JOSEPH WAS JESUSes
DAD, THEN ARE YOU
HIS GRANDPA?

SARA AGE 6

The angel Gabriel said to Mary, the mother of Jesus:
"The baby born to you will be utterly holy —
the Son of God."

LUKE 1:35 (TLB)

Dear God,
    If I have friends that don't go to heaven will I still be able to remember them?
    Love,
      Jonathan (age 8)

Dear God,

Why does it rain so much in April? The grass is pretty long, but I can't mow it, because it's raining.

Catherine (age 12)

He gives us autumn and spring rains
in their seasons. He makes sure we have the
harvest at the right time.

JEREMIAH 5:24 (ICB)

Dear God,

Will I ever see my Grandpa again?

Misty (age 8)

For God so loved the world,
that He gave His only begotten Son,
that whoever believes in Him should not perish,
but have eternal life.

JOHN 3:16 (NAS)

Dear God,
How do you know when it's time
for someone to go up to heaven?

Ashley (age 11)

All the days planned for me
were written in your book before
I was one day old.

PSALM 139:16 (ICB)

Dear God,
How many Angels are in the Angel choir?

Paul 9

But you have come to Mount Zion
and to the city of the living God, the heavenly Jerusalem,
and to myriads [ten thousands] of angels.

HEBREWS 12:22 (NAS)

Dear God,
Where do animals go when
they die?? do they go to
People heaven??

Sara
(Age 9)

Whatever is good and perfect
comes to us from God, the Creator of all ...

JAMES 1:17 (TLB)

Dear God,
when I die and
go to heaven,
how do I get
up to heaven?
Katherine (age 9)

Jesus said: "After I go and prepare a place for you,
I will come back. Then I will take you to be with me
so that you may be where I am."

JOHN 14:3 (ICB)

Dear God,
Will I have to sleep in
heaven? I hope not.
WILLS (age 5)

And there shall no longer be any night.

REVELATION 22:5 (NAS)

Dear God,
    When will you come back?

                    Zachary (age 8)

No one knows the date and hour
when the end will be — not even the angels.
No, nor even God's Son. Only the Father knows.

MATTHEW 24:36 (TLB)

Dear God,

Will I go to Heaven when I die?
I certainly hope so!

Gillian
(age 12)

All things are possible to him who believes.

MARK 9:23 (NAS)

Dear God,
How many hairs are on everybodies head alltogether?

Jared age,9

Dear God
Why is there a devil?
Jessica
(age 8)

How you are fallen from heaven, O Lucifer,
son of the morning! How you are cut down to the ground —
mighty though you were against the nations of the world.
For you said to yourself, "I will ascend to heaven and
rule the angels. I will take the highest throne.
I will preside on the Mount of Assembly far away
in the north. I will climb to the highest heavens and
be like the Most High." But instead, you will be brought
down to the pit of hell, down to its lowest depths.

ISAIAH 14:12-15 (TLB)

Dear God,
How did you make the world in just 7 days?

Christie
(Age 8)

Praise him, sun and moon.
Praise him, all you shining stars.
Praise him, highest heavens and you waters above the sky.
Let them praise the Lord because they were created by his
command. He set them in place forever and ever.
He made a law that will never end.

PSALM 148:3-6 (ICB)

Dear God,
Do you have to wear shoes in heaven? I see pictures of angels but I never see them wearing shoes.

Aaron
(age 7)

Dear God,

How did you be Created if there was nothing here in the begining of time.

Valerie age 9

Now I know only a part.
But at that time I will know fully, as God has known me.

1 CORINTHIANS 13:12 (ICB)

Dear god, I like you alot
but I want to ask you
a little question.

When I go to heaven will
I be an angel? if I am
where would I get my
clothes and where would
I get my wings fitted?
or my halo?

Ben   (age 8)

For we know that when this tent we live in now is
taken down — when we die and leave these bodies —
we will have wonderful new bodies in heaven, homes that will
be ours forevermore, made for us by God himself, and
not by human hands. . . . That is why we look forward eagerly
to the day when we shall have heavenly bodies which we
shall put on like new clothes. For we shall not be merely
spirits without bodies. . . . We want to slip into our
new bodies so that these dying bodies will, as it were,
be swallowed up by everlasting life.

2 CORINTHIANS 5:1-4 (TLB)

Dear God,
When you go to heaven,
can you bring one thing
from Earth?

Kelley (age 8)

Dear God,
Why are there so many people that want to kill other people?

Ashley (age 10)

...man's bent is always toward evil
from his earliest youth ...

GENESIS 8:22 (TLB)

Dear God,
   How big is heaven? As big as a football field or larger?

                    Ben [age 9]

Dear God,
Why can't I ever see you?
I've prayed to you every
day since I was a little
girl but I would like
to see you and
give you a hug.
Hannah (age 6)

We can see and understand only
a little about God now, as if we were peering
at his reflection in a poor mirror; but someday
we are going to see him in his completeness,
face to face.

1 CORINTHIANS 13:12 (TLB)

Dear God,
Why do you let bad things happen?

Beth (Age 10)

Jesus said: "The thief's [devil's] purpose is to steal, kill and destroy. My purpose is to give life in all its fullness."

JOHN 10:10 (TLB)

Dear God,

How old are you?

Jason (age 7)

I am the Alpha and the Omega,
the First and the Last, the Beginning and the End.

REVELATION 22:13 (ICB)

Dear God,
   Do you have to work for your money in heaven?

Michelle (age 9)

They shall rest from all their toils and trials;
for their good deeds follow them to heaven!

REVELATION 14:13 (TLB)

Dear God,

Are all the streets made of gold or just some of them? Is everyone rich up there? I would Like to Be rich

IVY (age 8)

And **the street** of the city was pure gold,
like transparent glass.

REVELATION 21:21 (NAS)

. . . and your blood has bought people from
every nation as gifts for God.

REVELATION 5:9 (TLB)

Dear God,

My great grandad is about to die. He, being 96, is not in good shape. Once he is in Heaven will he be strong again?

Christi (age 11)

God himself will be among them.
He will wipe away all tears from their eyes,
and there shall be no more death, nor sorrow,
nor crying, nor pain. All of that has gone forever.

REVELATION 21:3,4 (TLB)

Dear God,
   will I have a whirl pool
in my place in heaven?
         Sara
         (age 9)

Dear God,
Why did you make
tornadoes and
lightning?

William
(age 5)

He makes mists rise throughout the earth
and sends the lightning to bring down the rain.

PSALM 135:7 (TLB)

Dear God,

Why did you make us?

Lauren (age 8)

God said, "Let us make a man — someone like ourselves,
to be the master of all life upon the earth and
in the skies and in the seas."

GENESIS 1:26 (TLB)

I will walk among you and be your God,
and you shall be my people.

LEVITICUS 26:12 (TLB)

57

Dear God,
I really like to run and play all kinds of sports and super Nintendo. Is that going to be OK with you?
Ian (age 11)

Enjoy serving the Lord.
And he will give you what you want.

PSALM 37:4 (ICB)

Dear God,
Do any bad people go to heaven?

Robert (age 10)

Nothing evil will be permitted in it —
no one immoral or dishonest — but only those whose
names are written in the Lamb's Book of Life.

REVELATION 21:27 (TLB)

Dear God,

Why are people so greedy
And care more about
money and fight over
stupid things?

Evan
(age 9)

The love of money causes all kinds of evil.

1 TIMOTHY 6:10 (ICB)

Dear God,

How many malls are in heaven?

Amy (age 13)

Dear God,
   What is my guarding
angel's name?
                    Lauren (age 9)

Dear God,
Is there church in
heaven?

Britta age 8

No temple could be seen in the city,
for the Lord God Almighty and the Lamb are
worshipped in it everywhere.

REVELATION 21:22 (TLB)

65

Dear God,

Did my cat Fuzzball go up to heaven? Is he happy? He liked to play with me. Would you please play with him?

Joy (age 10)

Dear God,
How do you get around in heaven? I know that angels fly because I've seen pictures of them and they have wings, but I've never seen a picture of you.

Samuel (age 4)

He walks upon the wings of the wind.

PSALM 104: 3 (NAS)

Dear God,

Do I have a guardian angel? I don't know if I really need one since I have a Mom and Dad and Nana and Papa and Grammy and Granddad who take care of me.

Elizabeth (age 4)

Jesus said: "Beware that you don't look down upon a single one of these little children. For I tell you that in heaven their angels have constant access to my Father."

MATTHEW 18:10 (TLB)

Dear God,

The earth is so small and the universe is so big. Is there life in some other part of the universe? Is there such a thing as an alien?

Laurel (age 10)

And the living beings ran to and fro like bolts of lightning.

EZEKIEL 1:14 (NAS)

God can do much, much more
than anything we can ask or think of.

EPHESIANS 3:20 (ICB)

Dear God,
    When we die and go to Heaven do we turn into angels or are we just regular people?
              Your Servant,
                 Christi (age 12)

Don't you realize that we Christians will
judge and reward the very angels in heaven? So you should
be able to decide your problems down here on earth.

1 CORINTHIANS 6:3 (TLB)

Dear God,
  Can I ride in a
fire chariot when I
get to heaven?
            Adam
            (age 6)

And everything you ask in prayer,
believing, you shall receive.

MATTHEW 21:22 (NAS)

Dear God,
    If we all have a mansion in heaven, will we have to clean it?

                Brooke Age-13

Dear God,
Will we wear a bright white robe in
Heaven because I would love
to wear one.

Keisha (age 8)

Let us be glad and rejoice and honor him;
for the time has come for the wedding banquet of the Lamb,
and his bride has prepared herself. She is permitted to wear
the cleanest and whitest and finest of linens. (Fine linen
represents the good deeds done by the people of God.)

REVELATION 19:7,8 (TLB)

Dear God,
Where was I before
I was born?

Jonathan (age 6)

You made my whole being.
You formed me in my mother's body.

PSALM 139:13 (ICB)

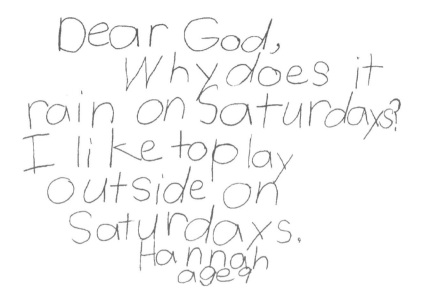

Dear God,
Why does it rain on Saturdays? I like to play outside on Saturdays.
Hannah
age 9

There is a right time for everything . . .

ECCLESIASTES 3:1 (TLB)

Dear God,
   Are there any farms up in heaven, or just one big city? Is there just one city or are there other towns?

                Kyle (age 11)

And I know how such a man — whether in the body or apart from the body I do not know, God knows — was caught up into Paradise, and heard inexpressible words, which a man is not permitted to speak.

2 CORINTHIANS 12: 3,4 (NAS)

Dear God,
    Will I see my great great grandmother in heaven because I never saw her? How will I know its her?

    Jermaine (age 8)

Now I know only a part. But at that time
I will know fully, as God has known me.

1 CORINTHIANS 13:12 (ICB)

Dear God,

Can you call people on the phone when you are in heaven?

Shamar (12 age)

Dear God,

What do you look like, God?

Brent (age 11)

Jesus said:
"He who has seen me has seen the Father."

JOHN 14:9 (ICB)

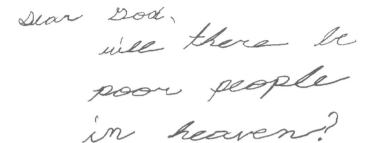

Dear God,
will there be
poor people
in heaven?

Dylan (age 9)

It is time to reward your servants
the prophets and to reward your holy people.

REVELATION 11:18 (ICB)

To him who overcomes
I will grant to sit with Me on My throne.

REVELATION 3:21 (NKJV)

Dear God,
Do I have to go to school in heaven?

Mickey (age 9)

Now we have received, not the spirit of the world,
but the Spirit who is from God, that we might know the
things freely given to us by God . . .

1 CORINTHIANS 2:12 (NAS)

Dear God,
      Do YOU go to church
every Sunday?

                Jamie
                (age 10)

Dear God,

How can you live everywhere in the world but no one can see you?

Greg (age 8)

The Lord looks down from heaven.
He sees every person. From his throne he watches
everyone who lives on earth. He made their hearts.
He understands everything they do.

PSALM 33:13-15 (ICB)

Dear God,
DO you live iN a
castle? If
you do I would
like to visit.
  Erika (age 6)

It had a great and high wall, with twelve gates,
and at the gates twelve angels . . .
And the wall of the city had twelve foundation stones,
and on them were the twelve names of the
twelve apostles of the Lamb.

REVELATION 21:12,14 (NAS)

Dear God,

Will I still have to move alot in heaven? If I do it's fine as long as I can take my friends with me. I miss my friends.

Charlene (age 11)

Dear God,
  If there are roads
up in heaven, are
there any cars that
can drive on them?
How fast do they go?

          Grant (age 8)

Dear God,

Do you Love me God?

I Love you?

I think you do?

Jenna (Age 8)

And from far away the Lord appeared to his people.
He said, "I love you people with a love that will last forever.
I became your friend because of my love and kindness."

JEREMIAH 31:3 (ICB)

What question do you have for God?

We'd love to hear from you.

You can write us at:

HONOR BOOKS
P. O. Box 55388
Tulsa, Oklahoma 74155